VICTORIA
ANOTHER VIEW

for lee and Irene..

ROBERT AMOS

victoria 2000

ORCA BOOK PUBLISHERS

Canadian Catalogue in Publication Data

Amos, Robert, 1950-
   Victoria: another view

   Includes index.
   ISBN 1-55143-005-3
   1. Victoria (B.C.) in art.   2. Victoria (B.C.) — Description and travel.   I. Title
FC3846.37.A46 1993   917.11'28'0022
F1089.5.V6A46 1993   C93-091634-4

We gratefully acknowledge the financial assistance of The Canada Council.

Photography by M. Sarah Amos
Book design by Robert Amos and M. Sarah Amos
Cover design by Susan Fergusson

Printed and bound in Hong Kong

Orca Book Publishers
PO Box 5626, Station B
Victoria, BC
Canada V8R 6S4

Orca Book Publishers
Box 3028, 1574 Gulf Road
Point Roberts, WA
USA 98281

To contact the artist:
Robert Amos
1129 McKenzie Street
Victoria, BC
Canada V8V 2W1

Dedicated to Sarah,
who took the photographs and provided peace of mind

Introduction

Eleven years ago, when our eldest child was one, my husband and I decided we should hole up in a hotel suite in Victoria for two weeks while the interior of our house in White Rock was painted. As it turned out, this was disastrous for the house — our painter seemed to have obtained his colour wheel from the Star Trek School of Design. However, it was good for us, as it began our long-standing love affair with Victoria.

We have returned faithfully almost every year, usually in February or March, much to the bewilderment of those who regard this practice as something akin to summering in Siberia. "You could go to Palm Springs," they say. (Now there's a truly terrible place — wealth without wit, glitz without glamour, artifice without art. Where Bob Hope lives. Where Liberace died.) "If not Palm Springs, at least somewhere exotic."

However, as far as we are concerned, Victoria *is* exotic. In Victoria we can sense the almost palpable presence of the Empire and the people who traversed it — who arrived with steamer trunks covered with labels from places in the Near and Far East. And of rich lives unwinding slowly during gentler times.

We always treat ourselves to brunch at the Oak Bay Beach Hotel, which has not only the same menu every year but the same patrons too — a retired British Army major, an Anglican minister, a fresh-faced civil servant in a Shetland sweater. And then there is the Blethering Place Tea Room, which supports my theory that a place of true character always has mismatched chairs . . .

During one of our early visits I bought my first Amos card. It was *Government Street in the Rain*. Subsequently, I bought an Amos card to commemorate every visit and soon had a small collection. There may be more architecturally accurate renderings of Victoria available, but for me Robert's evocative pictures truly capture the atmosphere of the place.

I was really pleased when *Victoria by Robert Amos* appeared in my local bookstore. Here were pages and pages of the "cards" and also the voice of the person who made them. And here was Victoria, a city of nooks and crannies and quaint buildings constructed to a human scale. Victoria is so irregular, with real neighbourhoods and a wonderful aura of slight dereliction . . . and, at the end of the day, those remarkable evening skies.

I wrote to Robert to express my appreciation, and thus began a wonderful friendship between our families. And now here I am writing the introduction to his next book.

It is tempting to become the aggressively dull art historian and do a thorough analysis of Robert's work, but he doesn't seem to like that practice and probably would prefer to let the paintings speak for themselves. Which they do most eloquently. Obviously we've "got the message," which occurred because the medium is totally appropriate to the task. Watercolour nicely captures the ephemeral qualities of Victoria, and Robert's peculiarities of perspective convey its beloved irregularity.

His influences have been outrageously eclectic, and he might be compared in that respect to a whale, feeding indiscriminately and sifting out whatever interesting things happen along through the baleen of his perceptions.

He leaves philosophy to the philosophers. Even so, if you look at Robert's work for any length of time, you will soon discover his basic principle, that the everyday can be exotic. In his paintings he shows us his deep appreciation for the cosmic beauty of the commonplace.

Arla J. Swift,
White Rock, B.C.

From the Artist

Some time ago, when I set out to be a professional, full-time artist, I wondered about the focus of my work. It occurred to me that no one was seriously considering the image of this city, though we often say its beauty attracts us.

In the past, other artists have painted Victoria. The Spanish and English explorers brought artists, and later the daughters of the colonists went on sketching picnics. In the 1940s and 1950s, Edward Goodall resided here and painted postcards and calendar scenes as an adjunct to his work for the *Illustrated London News*. When I began my work in Victoria in 1975, the city seemed to be inundated with artworks fresh from the Inside Passage or the south of France, but our City of Gardens was without its champion.

At that stage in my artistic development I

Near Bay Street Bridge

decided that if I painted what things really looked like, the future would want to preserve my paintings simply as a record, whether I was judged to be a good painter or not. Let them be "antiques of the future." To that end, I have avoided the carefully preserved heritage structures in favour of things which look "ordinary" and are soon to disappear. In these changing times, the present is often soaked with the atmosphere of the soon-to-be-passé.

I am more interested to include things in my pictures than to edit them out. I have always put in lots of cars, not only because they are everywhere, but because they date the pictures so quickly. For years I was shy about drawing people, worried that my vision was too "cartoony" and would destroy some of the elegance I thought I should be striving for. I have thought better of that and now take courage from the expressionist example of Maxwell Bates.

In this book, I have not included the individual houses and stores which I paint on commission. I usually have a commission ahead of me, a scene to paint as a wedding gift or to commemorate some other event. I welcome the interaction that this type of work brings between the client, the subject and myself.

Anything could be fitting subject matter for me — gas stations, drive-in restaurants, backyards and sidestreets are all part of my vision. As I go about the town, different perspectives and seasons, times of day and changes of lighting all press themselves upon my attention. There's enough here for more than one lifetime.

In my travels, my slightly twisted style of realism has been applied to Vancouver's Chinatown, to Britain, Japan, Thailand and the area around my family's summer place in Muskoka. Someday my curious portraits of "eminent Victorians" will be discovered. But for now let's keep the focus on Victoria, a well-loved and surprisingly little-known city.

Influences

Art writers often mention the names of other artists, better known, whose work bears some sort of resemblance to the work of the artist under consideration. To forestall this speculation, I have made a list of artists whose work has some direct and tangible bearing on the paintings in this book.

Basically my intentions are found at the nexus of three fields of art. These are the British topographical watercolourists, the "floating world" of Japanese printmakers, and the example of a number of Canadian artists whose works deserve to be better known. Here are some artists to whose work I look for inspiration:

Japanese printmakers Hokusai, Hiroshige, Hasui: at first it was the complex compositions which attracted me to Hokusai, so different from the "vanishing point" perspective which pervades western art. Later I came to appreciate the day-to-day subject matter of Hiroshige's "floating world." Eventually, it was artists of the 1930s, the most influential being Hasui, who had most to say to me. They had western training, tempered it with a Japanese mood, and presented the image in the technically sublime medium of coloured woodcut print.

Rembrandt: his drawings and etchings show how a few lines and a Zen-like attention can convey a great deal about life as it goes on around us.

Henri Matisse: a colourist, a stay-at-home artist, and one who continues to delight. Despite the simple means, the mystery of his work is never completely dispelled.

William Hogarth: his curiosity about the life of his times is unparalleled, and he could draw — everything.

Herald Street

J.M.W. Turner: as a teenager Turner was the best topographical sketcher ever. Through a long career he drew and painted watercolours on the spot wherever he went. His techniques for catching sky effects, for drawing entire cities dissolving in a heat haze, and his use of gouache on blue-grey paper are inspiring.

John Sell Cotman: a contemporary of Turner, he was the master of the pure watercolour style, based on extremely effective designs executed in broad flat washes of colour.

Samuel Palmer: as a young man Palmer fell under the influence of William Blake, and went to the countryside where he painted rapturous views of the land. I appreciate the obsessive and rather psychedelic effects of his early work.

Stanley Spencer: an English artist, Spencer is most famous for his religious work, essentially painted Passion Plays in which he set Biblical narratives in his home village of Cookham. Spencer also painted "pot-boilers" throughout his life, recording the mundane details of Cookham with love and patience, and this work deserves to be better known.

David Hockney: an enormously creative artist, Hockney first attracted me with his coloured pencil works. Through the accessible and fascinating books filled with reproductions of his art and transcriptions of his speech, I came to admire his working methods. He is one of the best portraitists alive today, a splendid printmaker, and his approach to photography revolutionizes the medium.

Edward Hopper: I am not in sympathy with Hopper's atmosphere of urban isolation, but his subject matter, the ordinary facts of city and suburban life, has been quite influential for me. His watercolour style, in particular, has sometimes served as a model.

Emily Carr: anyone painting on the Canadian west coast recognizes the vision of Miss Carr on a regular basis, and we are the better for it.

In the beginning she painted in a documentary way. Her watercolours got larger and larger and she was not fussy about finish. In mid career she incorporated fauve style and colours. Finally, she dedicated all her work to transcendence through painting the landscape. She is an excellent and useful example, accessible through her extensive writings.

David Milne: while I can't make my work resemble his, there is much to learn from Milne's approach to subject, his brilliant compositional sense, his willingness to work all his life on a small scale, and his restrained and elegant colour sense.

Jack Shadbolt: this artist grew up in Victoria. While most of his later work comes from a stimulus I don't share, in the late 1940s he drew and painted the street life of Victoria and Vancouver. The scene of ghosts and goblins out on Robson Street on Hallowe'en night sticks in my mind, a combination of mood, document and caricature which is a rich vein of subject matter for any artist.

E. J. Hughes: an artist from this area who got a proper training in Vancouver, Hughes worked in a social realist style on murals and war records up till about 1946. Then he began a careful, colourful and well-composed record of southern Vancouver Island which shows us this region in a new way.

William Kurelek: a man compelled to paint what he knew, all the parts of his life. Kurelek was basically a self-taught, utterly direct painter who used the means at hand to describe dramatic scenes, and always placed people at the centre. His paintings were anecdotal and illustrative. Kurelek was enormously productive, which I take to be a good sign in an artist.

Maxwell Bates: an artist from Calgary who lived for years in Victoria at the end of his life, Bates most often painted people. He did so with a "take it or leave it" attitude that has given me confidence to put people in my paintings. For Bates, an elegant surface to his picture was less important than the subject, which was almost always the human condition.

Jack Wise: Wise paints with gouache and ink as well as watercolour and helped me break out of the strictures associated with "pure watercolour." Wise is influenced by the opaque colours of Tibetan painting, the calligraphic force of Chinese painting and the meditational mysticism which will show a painter where to leave his mind while he paints. Wise told me "painting is a study for more than one lifetime."

About My Technique

In my previous book, *Victoria by Robert Amos*, I included a description of who I am and how I painted the pictures. Things haven't changed much, so I'll say the same again.

I was born in Belleville, Ontario, in 1950 and grew up in Toronto. Though I graduated from the Fine Art Program of York University there, it wasn't until I came to Victoria that I really began to paint in the style which this book presents.

From 1975 until 1980 I was Assistant to the Director of the Art Gallery of Greater Victoria and during that time I was able to examine thousands of paintings and prints at first hand. The topographical paintings by British watercolourists of the eighteenth and nineteenth centuries suggested a direct approach to the landscape, and soon I bought my first box of watercolour paints, a pocket set smaller than my hand.

Armed with this and one tiny brush, on weekends I set out on my bicycle to find a way to respond to the beauty of Victoria. Subject matter was all around me — sunsets, islands, ferryboats, scenes on the beaches. For the first couple of years I explored the shorelines of

Oak Bay and Fairfield.

Soon the limits of my practice became all too apparent. My one tiny brush necessitated a sort of pointillism, and the purist approach to watercolour — all transparent, with no black or white paint — was hobbling my creativity. Fortunately a year of study with Jack Wise at the Victoria College of Art set me right. He introduced me to gouache, an opaque paint like poster paint, which provided the strong colours I was eager to use.

This bright and portable sketching technique was perfect for the travelling artist, and when I spent a year sketching and painting in Japan and Thailand, my style developed rapidly. I found enough colour there — violet, purple and citron — and I also enjoyed painting with fifty people looking over my shoulder. Later, on the quiet and well-mannered streets of Victoria, I missed the chorus of "very good!" and "what's your name?" after every brush stroke.

Back in Victoria, I decided to try painting my hometown as if it too were exotic. Chinatown was my home at first, site of the new Gate of Harmonious Interest and a lot of neon lights. After painting Fisgard Street in its entirety, I moved on to the Parliament Buildings and the Inner Harbour, and since then have been painting the whole town, bit by bit.

I have exhibited in many commercial galleries here, and a number of my paintings of the construction of the Victoria Conference Centre were purchased by the City. In 1984 I was made an Honourary Citizen of the City of Victoria for my painting and for the art writing which I have published on a weekly basis since 1981.

In my neighbourhood I have become a familiar sight, pulling the red wagon which, like Emily Carr's baby buggy, holds art supplies. Unpacking my paper (stretched and stapled on a board) and a stool to sit on, I begin drawing with an HB pencil.

Wiggly is better than straight, it seems. The distortions of perspective that creep into my drawings are to be encouraged, not corrected. On a simple armature of pencil lines, I flood in the colours, enjoying the unpredictability of watercolour paints. This kind of painting is a sort of "high-wire act." Sometimes I inscribe the salient features with a scratchy old steel pen dipped in a bottle of Chinese ink. Successive applications of paint bring the image into focus, and I continue either until I am satisfied or else I am too chilled to go on.

Later, in the comfort of my studio, I continue to elaborate details only suggested on the spot. The texture of coloured pencils on top of the watercolours is sometimes added into the mix. What began quickly slowly draws to a conclusion over days, weeks — sometimes years.

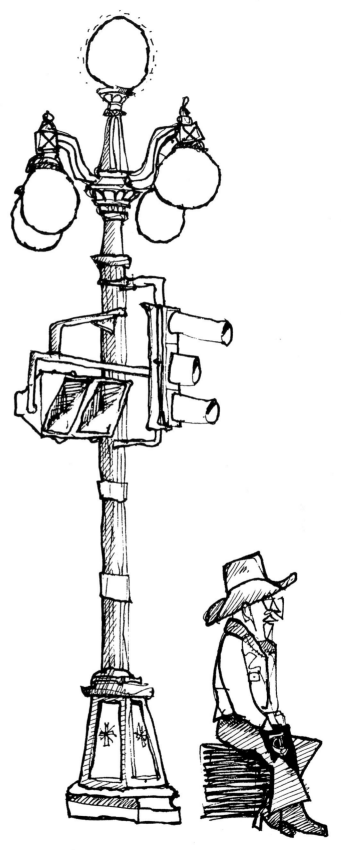

List of Plates

The Plates

A snowfall in Victoria goes beyond the meteorologically mundane — it is an Act of God, and as such requires the suspension of such prosaic activities as showing up for work or having your teeth cleaned. In the winter, Victoria is usually a few square miles of soggy cornflakes, the thin mush of trampled autumn leaves soaked by intermittent rains. Situated on a low-lying promontory on the seaward side of the Coastal Range of mountains, Victoria is spared the socked-in drizzle which plagues Vancouver in the winter. Here, we are swept by westerly winds which alternately pelt us with showers and then blow away the clouds to reveal an open blue sky. If you don't like the weather, wait fifteen minutes!

At least once in every winter our weather pattern reverses. When the wind swings over to the east, we are in for a freezing. It's as if someone left the back door open on the rest of Canada, a refrigerator door at that. Then, the snow comes: thick fluffy flakes created just at the freezing point.

Appointments are cancelled, timid drivers stay home, and the curious come out to enjoy the change of scenery. All manner of moth-balled sleds and toboggans are brought out of the attic for a day of sliding down Beacon Hill. Ladies stroll about under umbrellas, a sight never seen in a Calgary snow storm. And just when winter becomes drudgery, the wind shifts and it's back to snowdrops and crocuses again.

I painted the Chinese Public School on a sunny winter day. As architectural historian Martin Segger has said, the school is " . . . a riot of unbridled Victorian eclecticism barely restrained within the traditional and somewhat vague references to the pagoda form."

In about 1908, Lou-Poy, a respected farmer and retail fruit and vegetable dealer, wanted to send his sons to school. Neither their claim as native-born nor his claim as a land-owning taxpayer would convince the board to let them attend.

So the Chinese community took the school board to court. The Chinese Consolidated Benevolent Association gathered a defence fund of several thousand dollars. When their lawyer lost the case, he charged only a nominal fee and gave the balance to be spent on a site for a new Chinese School. By the time the school was opened in 1909, the school board had recanted and allowed Chinese Canadians to attend regular schools. But the new school was put to good use. Now the school teaches Canadians about Chinese culture.

Chinatown Public School (1908) on Fisgard Street, 1991   *265 x 360 cm*

79 Wellington Street in bloom with Olympics in the distance, 1991 *370 x 540 cm*

Summer in Victoria doesn't make one pant for the air-conditioner and lemonade. Other places may boast autumn leaves with more spectacular colouring. For real winter, you'll want to go where sleigh-bells jingle on a regular basis. But for springtime, Victoria is unbeatable.

The Christmas tree is scarcely taken down when Mother Nature begins a new seasonal round, a veritable parade of flowers. As the years go by I have learned snowdrop, primula, crocus, daffodil, tulip . . . but soon the profusion of blossoms outstrips my ability to memorize and after a bit I can't remember whether it's campanula or convolvulus which is crowding me off the sidewalk. Before I came to Victoria I was honestly unaware that trees blossomed!

Linden Avenue has hawthorns, interspersed with magnolia trees, planted all the way down from the Rockland hill and off toward the Olympic Mountains. Many city streets boast a carefully organized variety of flowering trees. Most famous are the cherry, many of which were imported from Japan in the 1930s. Over twenty varieties have been planted along sixty of Victoria's three hundred streets. In fact, these aren't real cherry trees at all, but an ornamental non-fruiting plum called *prunus*. Moss Street is probably the most gorgeous, and is planted with white *Yoshino* blooms alternating with pink *Kwanzan* trees which blossom two weeks later. The effect of coasting down this road on a bicycle amid the falling blossoms (what the Japanese call *sakura no yuki* — the cherry blossom snow) is . . . dreamy.

Linden Avenue in bloom from the rise above Richardson Avenue, 1990   *370 x 540 cm*

St. Ann's Academy with apple blossoms, 1991   *370 x 540 cm*

Christ Church Cathedral and YMCA on Courtney Street, 1993   *350 x 530 cm*

Fisgard Street looking west toward Government Street at twilight, 1991   *265 x 360 cm*

Victoria has a compact and attractive downtown which centres on the harbour. I live nearby and my business takes me to most corners of the area on a regular basis. For me, Chinatown on Fisgard Street is "mainstreet."

In the evening I approach, beckoned by the neon lights and the promise of a good meal. Fascinating merchandise spills out onto the sidewalks. Here are shops and alleys a century old which are truly architecture on a human scale.

Chinatown is no longer an ethnic enclave, a ghetto for bachelor workers who came here from south China. They came to Gold Mountain to dig the mines, build the railways, grow vegetables, wash clothes, wait on tables, do the gardening and a thousand other useful tasks. By now those men have died and their children have moved to the suburbs. Chinatown has been made over by creative types and, in studios up long flights of stairs, many of the city's best artists live in bohemian splendour.

Roof of the Chinese Public School, 1988   *265 x 175 cm*

Chinatown Lions, 1989 *545 x 730 cm*

Not so long ago Chinatown was decrepit and forgotten, a shabby street or two notable for peeling paint and overhead wiring. Then, in 1979, Dr. David Chuenyan Lai, a professor of geography at the University of Victoria, coordinated a survey of the area and pointed out that there had been a change in demographics as well as a new respect for the Chinese contribution to Victoria. The visible symbol of this regeneration is The Gate of Harmonious Interest, an authentic ceremonial archway fifty-five feet across and thirty-eight feet high which spans Fisgard at Government Street.

Erected in 1981, it is made of ceramic tiles imported from Taiwan on a steel structure built by the City Works crew. The handsome structure is fronted by stone lions presented to Victoria by her Chinese sister city, Suzhou.

Fisgard Street from Fan Tan Alley, 1991   *270 x 730 cm*

Embassy Cafe at twilight on Fisgard Street, 1991   *545 x 710 cm*

The Embassy Cafe is gone now, a fate that all too soon overtakes much of what I consider paintable. In its place is a restaurant with tablecloths and curtains on the window. Yet I have fond memories of the Embassy as the quintessential cafe. A few potted plants and a pair of ceramic guardian lions faced the street and gave some protection to the counter which ran the length of the cafe. Usually there was someone sitting on one of the round stools gazing vacantly over the plastic dome which covered the donuts.

For those waiting to meet friends or have a bowl of won ton, the opposite wall was lined with booths. No pasta or croissants, no *maître d'* hovering about to make you nervous — just the straight goods. If the Embassy had a house special, it might have been a cigarette, a cup of coffee and the morning newspaper.

Embassy Cafe in the morning, 1988   *545 x 710 cm*

Wing's Market, 1984 *296 x 342 cm*

Dick Joe was the proprietor of Wing's Market. As the heir to much real estate in Chinatown, he didn't really need to run a grocery store. Yet the store was open every day, its dark recesses filled with non-perishable goods.

Wing's Market was his place to stand, a front door through which his friends could come and meet him on his own terms, as he watched the neighbourhood go by.

It was Dick Joe who made Chinatown an artists' colony. When the bachelors from China died off or moved out, all that space on second and third floors was vacant. Due to the fire-marshal's code and the endless anxiety about what would happen if we ever had The Big Earthquake, all those spaces were, at that point, unrenovatable within any reasonable budget. So they were left vacant, full of the bunks and cubicles and primitive communal kitchens which had been part of their previous tenement realities. The artists did their own interior decorating and, in return for a low rent, didn't make any demands on the landlord.

The payoff is a vibrant, safe and creative community. As yet, gentrification has scarcely begun.

Kimbo Restaurant on Fisgard Street, 1991   *360 x 265 cm*

West end of Fisgard Street at night, 1982   *390 x 560 cm*

Don Mee at night, 1982   *360 x 265 cm*

Fisgard Street looking east, 1993   *370 x 540 cm*

Don Mee at night (sketch), 1982   *300 x 225 cm*

Rainy night in Chinatown, 1982   *270 x 380 cm*

I used to live in Chinatown in a studio above Fan Tan Gallery. The scene out the second-storey window showed the Don Mee Restaurant and the north side of Fisgard Street, as enchanting to me as the "million dollar view" of sunset on the hills or the mountains across the Straits.

Most of my painting, then and now, is done "on the spot." It's a technique that requires a certain abandon but imbues the result with a spirit and liveliness impossible to obtain in the studio.

To create the sketch of Don Mee I climbed out the window and perched on the fire escape in what I recall to be very chilly weather.

The scene of the Gate of Harmonious Interest was created on a rainy night from a vantage point between two cars parked in the darkness. Thus the colours were chosen from my memory of what was on the palette and, to render the painting visible even in the dark, I had to make them brighter than I might otherwise have done.

Sparkling Parliament, 1992   *360 x 265 cm*

Symphony Splash painted from the barge — after dark, 1992   *370 x 540 cm*

There is no mistaking the power of Francis Rattenbury's vision. His first project in Victoria was the Parliament Buildings (1893–1897), which he designed at the age of twenty-five! He continued the ensemble with the Empress Hotel (1907), the CPR Steamship Terminal (1924, currently the Wax Museum) and the Crystal Gardens (1925). This group of buildings was conceived in relation to the eventual setting he visualized surrounding the Inner Harbour. Hard to believe now, it was only a stinking tidal mudflat when he began. At the moment it is unquestionably the focus of our city.

Victorians are, by nature and by definition, insular. It is hard to inspire us to community activity, for we seem to prefer individual to group endeavours. Yet a few events every year bring us out in numbers. These include the start of the Swiftsure sailing race, and the Moss Street Paint-In, during which about 15,000

art-lovers stroll from the Art Gallery of Greater Victoria down to the waterfront and back, admiring the work of dozens of our most public artists who take up positions by the sidewalk.

Annually a crowd of unequalled numbers — estimated at about 40,000 — is drawn to the Inner Harbour on a summer evening to participate in the Symphony Splash. Victoria's famous symphony orchestra is ferried out to a huge barge moored in front of the Legislature and plays a concert of outrageously popular favourites. The massive audience picnics on the lawns and bobbles about in boats. The climax has traditionally been Tchaikovsky's *1812 Overture*, taken to new heights with fireworks and a cannonade resounding throughout the harbour. My picture was painted during the performance from a position between the tympani and the french horns.

Victoria Classic Boat Festival

On the first weekend in September the docks below the Empress Hotel are lined with wooden boats, the featured performers of the Classic Boat Festival. You can admire the paint and brass from up close as you file by with those who throng the docks all day long. For the purpose of painting, I prefer the Sunday morning sail-past. At 11 AM the boats leave the wharfs and parade out of the harbour as slowly as they can go, filling the usually quiet waterway with a festival of flags and horns and scenes of discreet merriment.

The slow pace is just right for me. There's a place at the foot of the Songhees lands in front of Ocean Pointe Resort with a rocky ledge just big enough for me to set up my easel and be out of the way. Then the boats go by at a speed slow enough to let me capture them if I'm quick. That way, the fussiness of detail which boat owners insist upon isn't possible, but the *joie de vivre* which is a natural result of this event is everywhere conveyed.

Classic Boat Festival — with the
steam tug *Master*, 1992   545 x 730 cm

Thunderbird Park showing the Empress and Conference Centre, 1991   *360 x 265 cm*

Birdcages Walk Confectionery, 1991   *190 x 150 cm*

Thunderbird Park is the site of a collection of totems of the various native nations. Many were carved under the direction of Kwakwakw'waka chief Mungo Martin, who built his own house in their midst in the 1950s. Every year it is used more and more for native ceremonies and dances. Framed beyond is the Conference Centre and the Empress Hotel, and around the corner, the Birdcages Walk Confectionery.

Sam's Deli and Government Street, 1992   *360 x 265 cm*

Scotty House on Government at Courtney Street, 1990   *270 x 380 cm*

Government Street is still the main street of Victoria. It fulfils the function of all main streets — it is a microcosm of the economic life of the city. Between the harbour and View Street, you come upon clothiers, eateries, a tobacconist, a confectioner, a tea merchant, a bookseller, purveyors of fine linens and china, specialty shops, souvenir stores and art galleries.

If you follow Government Street south to its logical conclusion you will pass the Empress Hotel, the harbour, the Royal British Columbia Museum, the Parliament Buildings, government offices, a residential area, Emily Carr's childhood home, a couple of corner stores and finally you will come to Beacon Hill Park and the ocean. You can walk it comfortably in a couple of hours with a stop for tea.

When summer comes to Victoria, the banners, the flower baskets and the red buses all come out. Then, the visitors arrive and begin their trek from the Empress Hotel up Government Street. In the first block is Sam's Deli, famous for soup and mountainous sandwiches which can be enjoyed at sidewalk tables.

In the next block is the extravagant mock-Tudor of the Scotty House, a shop full of gift wares, housed in what was formerly the Windsor Hotel. Odd to think that all that fake half-timbering in black and white covers up a charming English-scale brick structure, built in 1859, and reputed to be the first brick building in Victoria. It's a case of the bogus heritage covering up the real thing. Which heritage will the future save?

Union Club dining room, 1991 *340 x 235 cm*

The Union Club is a proper British-style men's club, one of the revered symbols of this city and a reassuring symbol of continuity.

As a guest on a luncheon visit I was told I could not bring my sketchbox into the dining room — a rule which dissuades workaholics from spoiling the atmosphere by propping open briefcases on the tables. But I did sneak in a little paint set and sketched this scene, while hiding my work on my lap under the linen tablecloth.

After port and Stilton, one is in the perfect mood for a post-prandial stroll up Government Street to E. A. Morris Tobacconist to select a Havana cigar from the walk-in humidor. Fire it up at the onyx lightolier in the centre of the shop and step out through the bevelled glass splendour of Thomas Hooper's 1892 storefront. Ah, Victoria! The period elegance of E. A. Morris is mirrored down the street by the architect's 1893 design for Roger's Chocolates' storefront.

E. A. Morris, 1992 *360 x 265 cm*

Pagliacci's on Broad Street, 1992   *360 x 265 cm*

La Petite Colombe on Broughton Street, 1992   *360 x 265 cm*

Shops on Fort Street near Government, 1992   *395 x 565 cm*

Former Bank of Montreal on Government Street, 1992   *730 x 545 cm*

The old banks of Victoria were designed to reflect that power and glory, with imposing facades, stately interiors and finishing of the best materials. The Bank of Montreal (1896) was designed by Francis Rattenbury just at the time when he had completed work on the Parliament Buildings. Its "chateau" style was later recapitulated for his Empress Hotel and other hotels owned by the Canadian Pacific Railway, one of the bank's biggest customers.

It is now the Ralph Lauren—Polo clothing store. And similar metamorphoses have befallen the other head offices of these great old banking institutions. The Royal Bank of Canada, a block to the south, has been extensively refitted and embellished. As Munro's Books, it is probably Canada's most handsome bookstore. The former Bank of British Columbia, an 1886 building said to demonstrate a superb mastery of Italianate ornamentation in the High Victorian idiom, is now The Spirit of Christmas, a theme boutique.

Three Churches on Quadra Street, 1991   *360 x 265 cm*

Strathcona Hotel from Stephen Lowe Gallery, 1991 *370 x 540 cm*

The Stephen Lowe Gallery is located in the striking, spacious and well-lit space in the northeast corner of the Victoria Conference Centre at Douglas and Humboldt streets. I have had exhibits of my paintings there annually and I like to attend them as much as possible. Never one to stand about waiting for things to happen, I usually have a painting on the go. This, like most of the scenes in this book, was done on the spot.

The views from the gallery are taken up, at the moment, with parking lots and kiosks for every car-rental chain in the business. This is where the bus lines service their coaches, and there is a semi-defunct antique car museum here too. I hope that, within a few years, those parking lots will be covered with theatres and concert halls and this street corner will be the busy hub of a new cultural precinct in the city.

Stephen Lowe Art Gallery, Douglas and Humboldt, 1991   *360 x 265 cm*

Swan's Hotel and Pub at Pandora Avenue and Store Street, 1992   *360 x 265 cm*

Cowichan Trading Co. on Government at Johnson Street, 1992   *360 x 265 cm*

Market Square, from Store Street looking up Johnson, 1991   *270 x 730 cm*

Market Square calls itself "The Heart of Old Towne," and rightly so. When Victoria was an important port in the last century, ships from all over the Pacific docked here. Whaling, sealing and the search for sea-otter furs were lucrative industries, and sailors from all nations were ready for a good time when they finally came into port. While the ships tied up to resupply on the docks below Wharf Street, the sailors would be paid off and let loose up Johnson Street.

Their first steps in Victoria led them to one of the endless supply of saloons, whorehouses, pawnshops and curio emporiums in this part of town. It was said that there were so many bars on Johnson Street that, if you were thrown out of one, you'd probably land in another.

Things are better now. After years of skid-road dereliction, the block of faded hotels between Pandora Avenue and Johnson, Government, and Store streets was bought up and renovated.

The centre of the block was cleared of the infill of sheds, trash middens and substandard buildings. In its place a sheltered plaza surrounded by wooden mezzanines grew up, making it one of the city's most charming shopping areas. Market Square is also the site of many festivals in the course of the year.

Wing Hing's Truck, 1992
265 x 360 cm

Here is Chinatown on the road. At the time of writing this, the green truck belonging to Mr. Wing Hing was the last of its kind still delivering vegetables door to door. When I first displayed this painting, many people were moved to reminiscence and told me that Wing Hing had delivered produce to their grandparents . . . in the same truck! These trucks, the market gardens and corner grocery stores have always been a part of the special flavour of Victoria.

Choy Wong's Truck, 1991
265 x 360 cm

Vancouver Street Grocery, 1991   *265 x 360 cm*

Cook Street Village — Pink Beret, 1992   *360 x 265 cm*

Cook Street — Pic-a-Flic, 1992   *370 x 540 cm*

The Cook Street Village near Beacon Hill Park is my neighbourhood. It has developed over the years under the spreading chestnut trees in a compact and user-friendly way. This is a pedestrian community where the sidewalks are alive with strollers full of babies and the wheelchairs and walkers pushed by the old folks — truly the homeland of the "newly wed and nearly dead."

Architecture and urban design have scarcely touched the higgledy-piggledy charm of the Cook Street Marketplace, an outdoor fruit and flower shop kept open early and late by the kindly proprietor. The post office and the drug store see most of us on a daily basis. Two independent grocers battle for our business in their shops, facing one another across Cook Street. Pic-a-Flic has a city-wide reputation as the best video shop of all.

No wonder would-be developers of other urban environments in the city mention the Cook Street Village as their model. But Cook Street Village would never happen with 600 underground parking spaces and a parade of chain stores. It's pedestrians, neighbours and trees that make it what it is.

Gorge Produce, 1991 *265 x 360 cm*

The owners of the Sunbrite Laundromat can't seem to understand why I keep painting pictures of their shop. People come from all over the city to do their laundry here. It's clean, busy, well-run and friendly. One day I saw a wedding couple — tuxedo and bridal gown — having their portrait taken at the front door. For some reason this place means something to a lot of people. Maybe, when it has been renovated out of existence, the owners will figure out what I was up to.

Sunbrite Laundromat, 1992 *360 x 265 cm*

Beacon Drive-In on Douglas Street, 1988 *280 x 640 cm*

The Beacon Drive-In is the last stop for ice-cream and burgers before the beach at Dallas Road or the gardens of Beacon Hill Park. This painting was commissioned by a couple who, every morning, ride across town on their bicycles for exercise. It is their habit to stop here for coffee at 7 AM and chat up the regulars. Thus, I had to get up early to catch them basking in the low, golden rays of morning light. You can see their bikes parked against the rail.

Until I tried to draw this building I had never considered its bizarre architecture. It's been there a long time. Will this one day be a "heritage listed building"? Modern zoning regulations would probably never have allowed it in the first place but since it is there, the Beacon Drive-In will probably keep on selling burgers and cones until judgement day.

Fountain and Willow, Beacon Hill Park, 1991   *540 x 365 cm*

Medieval Bridge, Beacon Hill Park, 1989   *360 x 265 cm*

Beacon Hill Park was set aside for the city by Sir James Douglas, the Chief Factor of Fort Victoria and the second Governor of the Colony. Development of the park in something like its present form began in 1889, when the design by John Blair, a gardener of Scottish origin, was put into practice. He was apparently inspired in his layout by Frederick Law Olmsted, who designed Central Park in New York. For those who seek a deeper appreciation of this seventy-seven hectare pleasure ground I recommend *Trees of Greater Victoria: A Heritage*, "a field guide to the arboreal riches of Greater Victoria."

Gonzales Weather Station, 1990   *359 x 260 cm*

The Chinese Cemetery, located just off the scenic drive at Harling Point, is a magic place. It is a tiny, unique geological zone, and is blessed by *feng shui*, the form of geomancy by which the Chinese people choose propitious points on the face of the earth. The altar table is set with food and gifts for the deceased and the two little chimneys carry smoke from burnt offerings to the heavens.

This beautiful site is overlooked by the Gonzales Weather Station, which stands high on a hill behind. Since I painted these pictures, the Weather Station has been encroached upon by condominiums. The cemetery has been surrounded by a chain link fence while negotiations are underway to turn every available space near it into building sites.

The Chinese Cemetery at Harling Point, 1988   *550 x 750 cm*

Winter Olympics from Dallas Road, 1988   *430 x 1080 cm*

"HMS Olympic" E. Robert Ames 1936

Oak Bay Village, 1988 *265 x 360 cm*

My brother refers to Oak Bay Avenue as "Oak Bay High Street" — a proper British sort of title for this quaint district. Life truly is different "behind the tweed curtain." There is a conservatism evidenced by clipped moustaches and well-pruned privet hedges. The Colonel retired from the colonial service or the matron with memories of the Raj are still well-known.

Oak Bay Beach Hotel, 1992   *360 x 265 cm*

Hatley Castle, known as Royal Roads, 1989   *360 x 200 cm*

Autumn comes late in Victoria, and lingers. Occasionally we get just the right combination of clear weather and sharp frosty nights to yield a colourful crop of autumn leaves. And if that cold snap does bring a shock to the yellow birches and red maples, I can think of nowhere better to enjoy the display than the Japanese gardens at Royal Roads. The Japanese garden is well-maintained, picturesque, and very tranquil. On the day I painted this picture I was the only visitor during the whole afternoon.

Royal Roads is a military officers' training college and must be just about the most deluxe university in the country. It was built as Hatley Castle, a home for the Dunsmuir family, who also built Craigdarroch Castle. Spacious lawns in English fashion run to the sea. The formal garden is set about with Italianate sculpture. But the best bit is the extensive Japanese-style water garden.

And after viewing the gardens, you can get a close-up, hands-on view of a tank, an anti-aircraft gun and a jet fighter plane.

Japanese Garden, Royal Roads, 1987   *360 x 265 cm*

Turner's By Night, Fort and Richmond, 1987   *375 x 545 cm*

As the nights grow long, the lights of the city take on a new prominence. In this picture of the corner of Fort Street and Richmond Avenue, the lighting effects were almost the entire subject for me. The interplay of light defines the mood of this place more than does the slightly curious architecture of the semi-circular corner.

Starlight or the generalized glow of streetlights reflecting off low cloud cover gives a glow which illuminates all below. Streetlights and headlights define the roadway, distinct from the greenish fluorescent glow emanating from the corner store. A bank of neon lights cast their colours up across the store's facade and flood the dull sidewalk with a pool of reflected light. It's hard to realize that a hundred years ago none of this would have been possible.

Don Mee in Snow, 1993   *540 x 370 cm*

Snow on McKenzie Street on Christmas morning, 1991   *176 x 235 cm*

The quiet street is McKenzie Street, my street. I painted the neighbours' Christmas lights and snow early Christmas morning, after my children had woken up and opened their stockings, but before the day had fully broken.

While my beloved Cook Street Village was seeing some buildings torn down and new ones built up, I was a bit anxious. But in fact the result has been very good. The architecture is sympathetic, the chestnut trees have all remained, and we even got a fine new clock on an Edwardian cast iron pillar.

Oxford Arms in snow, Cook Street, 1990   *360 x 265 cm*